Nine Fruits *of the* Spirit

A Bible Study on Developing Christian Character

Gentleness

Robert Strand

New Leaf Press

A Division of New Leaf Publishing Group

First printing: June 1999
Third printing: September 2009

ISBN-13: 978-0-89221-465-3
ISBN: 0-89221-465-1
Library of Congress Number: 99-64010

Cover by Janell Robertson

Printed in China

Please visit our website for other great titles:
www.newleafpress.net

For information regarding author interviews, please contact the publicity department at (870) 438-5288.

Contents

Introduction

There is an ancient story out of the Middle East which tells of three merchants crossing the desert. They were traveling at night in the darkness to avoid the heat of the day. As they were crossing over a dry creek bed, a loud attention-demanding voice out of the darkness commanded them to stop. They were then ordered to get down off their camels, stoop down and pick up pebbles from the creek bed, and put them into their pockets.

Immediately after doing as they had been commanded, they were then told to leave that place and continue until dawn before they stopped to set up camp. This mysterious voice told them that in the morning they would be both sad and happy. Understandably shaken, they obeyed the voice and traveled on through the rest of the night without stopping. When morning dawned, these three merchants anxiously looked into their pockets. Instead of finding the pebbles as expected, there were precious jewels! And, they were both happy and sad. Happy that they had picked up some of the pebbles, but sad because they hadn't gathered more when they had the opportunity.

This fable expresses how many of us feel about the treasures of God's Word. There is coming a day when we will be thrilled because we have absorbed as much as we have, but sad because we had not gleaned much more. Jewels are best shown off when held up to a bright light and slowly turned so that each polished facet can catch and reflect the light. Each of these nine jewels of character will be examined in the light of God's Word and how best to allow them to be developed in the individual life. That is how I feel about the following three verses from Paul's writings which challenge us with what their Christian character or personality should look like. Jesus Christ has boiled down a Christian's responsibility to two succinct commands: Love the Lord your God with all your heart, mind, soul, and body, and love your neighbor like yourself. Likewise, Paul the apostle has captured for us the Christian personality in nine traits:

> But the fruit of the Spirit is love, joy, peace, patience, kindness, goodness, faithfulness, gentleness, and self-control. Against such things there is no law. Those who belong to Christ Jesus have crucified the sinful nature with its passions and desires. Since we live by the Spirit, let us keep in step with the Spirit (Gal. 5:22–25).

At the very beginning of this study, I must point out a subtle, yet obvious, distinction. The "fruit" of the Spirit is a composite description of what the Christian lifestyle and character traits are all about — an unbroken whole. We can't pick only the fruit we like.

Unlocked in these nine portraits are the riches of a Christ-centered personality. The thrill of the search is ahead of us!

Gentleness

PRAOTES, (Greek), meaning: Gentle,
mild, meek, to be an
inwrought grace of the soul.

THE FRUIT OF THE
SPIRIT IS . . . GENTLENESS

GENTLENESS is not weakness! The truly meek person is one
whose life has been empowered by the Spirit of God which comes
from faith that has been energized by the Word of God!

> *It should be that of your inner self, the unfading beauty of a gentle and quiet spirit, which is of great worth in God's sight (1 Pet. 3:4).*

When Jesus described himself as being "gentle and humble in heart" (Matt. 11:29), he was not without humility. His was not a life marked by weakness or indifference to others' needs about him.

While living in Colorado, I was privileged to watch a bunch of wild horses that had been rounded up and culled out of one of the last of the free-roaming, wild horse herds in America. They were being unloaded from their trailers into a corral. As they were being handled, there was much wild-eyed looking about, bucking, and running about not knowing what to expect. Totally untamed, unbroken, wild, and of not much value, they were being prepared for "adoption." For a small fee and the proof that you could care for one of these and had some land on which they could pasture, anybody could adopt and train a wild mustang. They were beautiful to look at.

Later, I had the privilege of riding one of these mustangs which had been broken, tamed to accept a saddle, bridle, and a rider. This horse had been "meeked" so as to behave in a certain acceptable manner. It neck-reined perfectly; in fact, it had become meek enough so that a child could ride it. However, at no time had this mustang lost its power to run or carry a rider or to work cattle. What a picture of "gentleness" or "meekness."

Most people upon hearing the word gentleness or meekness tend to immediately think of a "Walter Mitty" type of character — not very desirable. This is a gross misunderstanding. Meekness is not weakness!

Michael Drury said: "Humility so often seems vaguely desirable, but not really attractive. It might get one to heaven, but it won't promote a raise in pay. It sounds somewhat spineless, incompatible with intellect and a vigorous spirit." In reality, the reverse may be true. Think of some of the figures from history which we normally associate with humility, and we discover that none of these were of timid nature: Moses, Jesus Christ, Lincoln, Gandhi, Einstein, Mother Teresa. Gentleness/meekness is not putting down of self with an affected false sense of humility, rather it is a tough, free, confident kind of characteristic. Very desirable. Meekness is first of all our attitude toward God and not man. When our attitude toward God is that of meekness, then, too, our attitude toward others will reflect the same kind of spirit. This is not a spineless kind of wandering-about in relationships, but a solid force which causes us to stand and do the will of God in the face of every obstacle.

This is one of the rarest of all the distinctively Christian graces. This is positively declared to be precious in the sight of God: "It should be that of your inner self, the unfading beauty of a gentle and quiet spirit, which is of great worth in God's sight" (1 Pet. 3:4).

HIS PLAN FOR ME

When I stand at the judgment seat of Christ
And He shows me His plan for me,
The plan of my life as it might have been
Had He had His way, and I see
How I blocked Him here, and I checked Him there,
And I would not yield my will,
Will there be grief in my Savior's eyes,
Grief, though He love me still?
He would have made me rich, and I stand there poor,
Stripped of all but His grace,
While memory runs like a hunted thing
Down the paths I cannot retrace.

Then my desolate heart will well-nigh break
With the tears that I cannot shed.

I shall cover my face with my empty hands,
I shall bow my uncrowned head.
Lord, of the years that are left me,
I give them to Thy hand:
Take me and break me, mold me to
The pattern Thou hast planned.
                              (Martha Snell Nicholson)

GENTLENESS IS NOT BEING A WIMP

The person who has been really "gentled" by God, who is in the image of God in meekness, is the person who is directed by God. The goal in this study is to allow the Spirit of God to work on our inner character, conforming us to the image of His Son in all aspects of life, including gentleness and meekness.

Our first study sets the record straight — gentleness is not to be confused with weakness! Read again the account of the triumphal entry into Jerusalem on the day we have called "Palm Sunday" from Matthew 21:1–17.

Why is it that many of us tend to equate a gentle person with being a weak person?

_____

_____

_____

What was the impact that the events of this had on the people of Jerusalem?

_____

_____

_____

How is the gentleness of Jesus shown in these events?

_____

_____

_____

_____

What is the significance of the usage of palm branches at His entering Jerusalem?

_____

_____

_____

_____

_____

_____

_____

Name the specific Old Testament prophet who spoke what is written in verse 5 about Jesus' entry into Zion:

_____

_____

_____

_____

When cared for, palms grew in Jerusalem, but not as easily as Jericho which was called the "City of Palms." The palm is used as a figure of the righteous enjoying their deserved prosperity. Palm branches are a symbol of victory (Rev. 7:9), and the Early Church used the palm to express the triumph of the Christian over death through the Resurrection. On those early tombs the palm is accompanied by the monogram of Christ, signifying that every victory of the Christian is due to this divine name and sign. The palms were used to welcome victors into a city.

Why were the crowds so happy to welcome Christ on Palm Sunday and ready to crucify him on the following Friday?

_____

_____

_____

_____

_____

What was the motive behind the sudden change as noted in verses 12–13?

_____

_____

_____

_____

_____

Many a popular word picture of Jesus presents Him as being "meek and mild." How and why do the actions of Jesus differ from this picture?

_____

_____

_____

_____

_____

_____

In the midst of drastic actions, how is the gentleness of Jesus still demonstrated?

_____

_____

_____

_____

_____

Contrast the reactions of the common people to that of the chief priests and teachers of the law.

_____

_____

_____

_____

_____

_____

And why were they so indignant?

_____

_____

_____

_____

_____

What are the lessons on gentleness you have learned through this biblical passage?

_____

_____

_____

_____

_____

Can you think of life situations where this kind of firm, tough love in action is more appropriate than a soft, quiet, gentle approach?

_____

_____

_____

_____

_____

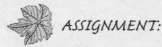 *ASSIGNMENT:*

• What steps are you taking so that you can achieve a gentleness that is not to be seen as a weakness?

_____

_____

_____

_____

• What person or persons in your life are in need of a tough, yet strong demonstration of gentleness?

_____

_____

_____

_____

_____

_____

How will you put this into action in that situation?

_____

_____

_____

_____

_____

GENTLENESS IN LEADERSHIP

Walk into any bookstore, browse through the internet, watch infomercials, and many are touting the same thing in their tapes, books, seminars, and training — look out for #1. You are being told that unless you learn how to swim with the sharks you'll never amount to anything, much less become a leader. Our society is obsessed with being aggressive, standing up for your rights, speaking out, and not being a wallflower. The contrast with what Jesus teaches on this subject is obvious. We have been told that to think like Jesus taught, that "the meek will inherit the earth," is out-of-date, hopelessly impractical, and

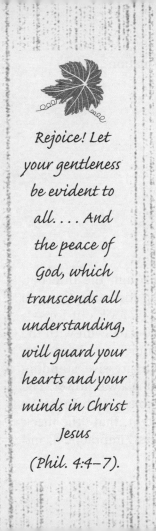

Rejoice! Let your gentleness be evident to all. . . . And the peace of God, which transcends all understanding, will guard your hearts and your minds in Christ Jesus (Phil. 4:4–7).

too naive for living and getting ahead in today's world.

To today's modern person, gentleness and meekness are not desirable character qualities. In contrast to that, there is hardly a single characteristic which you can name which will better distinguish the Christian from the rest of the world. We are being taught to think that the blessed are those who are strong enough to take from the weak, the shrewd, and those who refuse to be taken advantage of. It is people of such qualities who will be blessed with riches and strike success. We have set too high a premium on self-assertion. Gentleness is not a normal, native plant growing out of the human soul. It is not a natural part of our makeup. It grows as the Holy Spirit nurtures it. Meekness is to be part of your makeup no matter what your temperament might be or has been.

This next study takes us back to the Old Testament to take another look at one of the strongest leaders ever to emerge on the human scene. Please read Numbers 1:1–16.

Contrast the difference between weakness and meekness:

_____

_____

_____

_____

_____

Why were sister Miriam and brother Aaron so upset with their brother Moses?

_____

_____

_____

_____

_____

Let's go beyond the obvious — what were they really implying by their question?

_____

_____

_____

_____

_____

Who wrote verse 3?

_____

Why could this be said about Moses?

_____

_____

_____

_____

Why didn't Moses defend himself to his siblings?

_____

_____

_____

_____

_____

_____

What is God's opinion of the man Moses?

_____

_____

_____

_____

_____

_____

_____

Why do you think Miriam was punished and Aaron was not?

_____

_____

_____

_____

_____

_____

What lessons about gentleness and leadership did Miriam and Aaron need to learn?

_____

_____

_____

_____

_____

_____

What lessons of gentleness and meekness can you see from the life of Moses?

_____

_____

_____

_____

_____

_____

From the perspective of leadership, why do you think it's so hard for leaders to react in meekness?

_____

_____

_____

_____

_____

_____

What do you think were the lessons that the children of Israel might have learned from this situation (note verse 15)?

_____

_____

_____

_____

_____

Where and how did Moses learn to be "more humble than anyone else on the face of the earth"?

_____

_____

_____

_____

_____

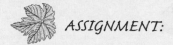 *ASSIGNMENT:*

• Have you ever been in a leadership situation, like Moses, where you obviously had the upper hand?

_____

_____

And how did you respond?

_____

_____

• What are the lessons in leadership you have gleaned from this passage?

_____

_____

_____

_____

GENTLENESS WITH OTHERS

The words gentleness and meekness are often confused in their meaning, and to add to this confusion, we have already done a study on "kindness." A definition is a bit elusive to pinpoint. In the original Greek language there are a number of words which can be translated "gentleness or meekness." It is more than an outward quality of words and deeds. Meekness tends to be emotional — it deals with how we feel within, while outwardly we may be acting gentle. Meekness has mostly to do with our spirit within. The Bible talks of the "spirit of meekness" (1 Cor. 4:21 or Gal. 6:1). It also speaks of the ornament of a meek and quiet spirit (1 Pet. 3:4). In actuality, only God can really discern what is happening in our spirit and appreciate what is happening within.

To be truly "feeling" submissive and humble might be lacking, but it's something which only each person knows. Outwardly we may be acting out a gentleness but on the inside there is a raging storm which has been covered. In any person's life, it's a Christian virtue not to show any kind of resentment — but it's an even deeper work of grace in the human heart not to "feel" any resentment of any kind. Jesus is the supreme example when He affirmed for all time, "I am gentle and humble in heart." Jesus was strength itself. It was not weakness but gentleness that was fulfilled when

"He did not open his mouth; he was led like lamb to the slaughter, and as a sheep before her shearers is silent, so he did not open his mouth" (Isa. 53:7).

In this next study, Jesus is the example of gentleness in Matthew 12:6–21.

What conclusions about Jesus have you come to after reading this passage?

_____

_____

_____

_____

_____

_____

_____

_____

_____

Come to me, all you who are weary and burdened, and I will give you rest. Take my yoke upon you and learn from me, for I am gentle and humble in heart, and you will find rest for your souls (Matt. 11:28–29).

Explain how "one greater than the temple" must have impacted his listeners.

_____

_____

_____

_____

_____

_____

How did Jesus show gentleness to the man with "a shriveled hand"?

_____

_____

_____

_____

_____

_____

How did he deal with the Pharisees on this occasion?

_____

_____

_____

_____

Why do you think so many who were sick followed Jesus?

_____

_____

_____

_____

Why do you think Jesus attracted such a following?

_____

_____

_____

_____

One of the truest tests of greatness is how a leadership person, or one who is in a superior position, treats others. From this passage, what can you draw about how Jesus treated those who might have been perceived to be a bit lesser than He?

_____

_____

_____

_____

_____

_____

From verse 18, how does he or how will he "proclaim justice to the nations"?

_____

_____

_____

_____

_____

What can we do as His followers today to proclaim justice?

_____

_____

_____

_____

_____

_____

Explain what "a bruised reed" and a "smoldering wick" represent to you:

_____

_____

_____

_____

_____

_____

How did Jesus respond to those who were physically sick, emotionally ill, or spiritually weak?

_____

_____

_____

_____

_____

_____

How did Jesus respond to those who felt they were superior to others, such as the Pharisees, teachers, and religious leaders?

_____

_____

_____

_____

_____

ASSIGNMENT:

• Generally, how do you respond to those around you who might be considered to be physically sick, emotionally hurting, lonely, abandoned, or without spiritual life?

_____

_____

_____

_____

_____

• What are some concrete steps you can take to insure a more gentle response on your part toward those in need?

_____

_____

_____

_____

GENTLENESS IN THE WORDS WE SPEAK

Maybe you've said it or heard kids shout it in defiance: "Sticks and stones may break my bones, but words will never hurt me!" Not! There have been many studies done about the sting of hurting words. Once spoken, words are almost impossible to retrieve. And how words can hurt! Spiteful words are weapons that can cut another to shreds. Too often we have spoken words that destroy young lives. Words that will be remembered over a lifetime.

Max Lucado penned these words: "Nothing is won by force. I choose to be gentle. If I raise my voice may it be only in praise. If I clench my fist, may it be only in prayer. If I make a demand, may it be only of myself."

Billy Graham wrote: "The word gentle was rarely heard before the Christian era, and the word gentleman was not known. This high quality of character was a direct by-product of Christian faith."

An enormous part of being considered a "gentle" person is measured by the words which we speak. This study takes us back to the wisdom of King Solomon. Let's read Proverbs 15:1–4, 25:11–15, and Matthew 11:28–30.

From Proverbs 15:1–4, what is revealed
to you about the power of words?

_____

_____

_____

_____

_____

Contrast what is considered "a gentle answer" to what "a harsh word" would be:

_____

_____

_____

_____

_____

_____

*The power of
the Holy Spirit
always will
function most
effectively and
divinely when it
has a background
of fruitful
gentleness in
the person who
exercises it.*

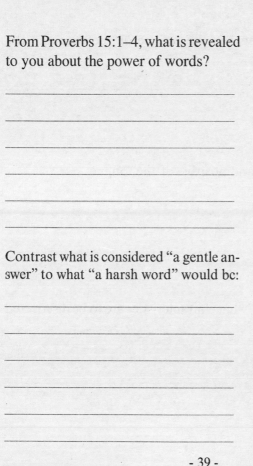

What's the difference between the tongue of the wise and the mouth of a fool?

_____

_____

_____

Talk about the negative and positive of the tongue:

_____

_____

_____

_____

From Proverbs 25:11–15, what characteristics are to be discovered about words?

_____

_____

_____

_____

What would be a word "aptly spoken"?

_____

_____

_____

_____

_____

_____

What analogies does this writer liken a word aptly spoken to?

_____

_____

_____

_____

_____

_____

What is the power of the gentle tongue?

_____

_____

_____

_____

From Matthew 11:28–29, what does Jesus invite us to do?

_____

_____

_____

_____

How would you explain taking his "yoke" upon you?

_____

_____

_____

_____

What can we "learn" from Him?

_____

_____

_____

_____

_____

_____

What is the difference between being "gentle" or "humble" in heart?

_____

_____

_____

_____

_____

_____

_____

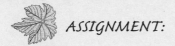

ASSIGNMENT:

• Write out your own working definition of gentleness:

_____

_____

_____

_____

• Are you faced with a real circumstance in your life in which you are called upon to show the real strength of gentleness?

_____

_____

_____

If so, how will you apply the lessons of this passage?

_____

_____

_____

_____

GENTLENESS AND POWER

Give me a gentle heart, that I may do
Naught but the gentle thing my whole life through.
Give me a heart as kind as heart can be,
That I may give before it is asked of me.
(Percy Thomas)

How many powerful people do you know whom you would consider also to be a gentle person? We've been socialized to believe that power corrupts and that total power totally corrupts. It can corrupt good manners, sensitiveness toward others, can cause arrogance, and can cause the recipient to selfishly look out for #1. An interesting study is to watch people as they climb the ladder of success and accumulate more power, and how they use or abuse it in their relationships with others.

A powerful person can also be a gentle person! But it may be more of a struggle. In this exhibit of gentleness, Jesus Christ is the supreme example. Never has there been a more powerful person who walked this earth. At His command were legions of angels, a Heavenly Father who had endued Him with deity. Demons fled at His command, sick bodies were healed with a touch or word — even nature could be subdued. Yet He did not flaunt it nor use it in any selfish ways. He never exploited others. He never threatened others with the powers at His command. He was powerful, yet gentle in character as well as in His actions.

One of the greatest tests in real life as to the reality of gentleness is to observe it when power is a part of the equation. There is a fine line that is drawn — you know when people are being kind out of obligation to impress others or it if is the real thing, done when no one else may be aware of what is taking place. Understand that as a fruit of the Spirit, gentleness is never the result of weakness. It requires great inner strength to be really gentle. People who are weak in character, when invested with a bit of power, are too often rough and unkind because they are weak. Such people despise gentleness in others as sign of weakness. Gentleness is really strength under control.

The true follower of God cannot know the extent of his/her gentleness so long as everything is moving along quite nicely with no bumps on the sea of life. But when the time comes that people mistreat you and the sea of life gets choppy, then the real test is on. Can I/you be gentle with others, then?

Blessed is the servant who doesn't think more highly of himself than he ought to when others are praising and promoting him as compared to the time in life when he was a virtual nobody.

Likewise, blessed is the servant who when rebuked can accept it humbly and with courtesy, always showing gentleness. Because:

> Where there is love and wisdom,
> There is neither fear nor ignorance.
> Where there is gentleness and humility,
> There is neither anger nor frustration.
> Where there is poverty with joy,
> There is neither greed nor covetousness.

You know, when we stop to think about it, this and all the other fruit of the Spirit have to do with our interactions with people, how we think of others, how we compare ourselves to others, and so on. The following has to do with gentleness in attitude of mind. It has to do with how we think of ourselves — the Bible tells us to not think more highly than we should. There's a balance to be struck. Just consider yourself most as you read this interesting piece:

THE OTHER FELLOW

When the other fellow takes a long time, he's slow.
When I take a long time, I'm thorough.
When the other fellow doesn't do it, he's lazy.
When I don't do it, I'm busy.
When the other fellow does something without being told,
He's over-stepping his bounds. When I do it, that's initiative.
When the other fellow overlooks a rule of etiquette, he's rude.
When I skip a few rules, I'm original.
When the other fellow pleases the boss, he's an apple-polisher.
When I please the boss, it's cooperation.
When the other fellow gets ahead, he's getting the breaks.
When I manage to get ahead,
       that's just the reward for hard work.

(Author is unknown)

And so it goes on, round and round, in this thing of human relationships. It's so easy to overlook or rationalize our own behavior, favorably I might add, to another's disadvantage. Gentleness is about being gentle at all times in all circumstances with all people.

For our last study on gentleness, please read from James 3:13–18 and 2 Corinthians 10:1–11.

Please write out your definition of what it means to be full of wisdom:

_____

_____

_____

_____

Let me ask the same question as James does, "Who is wise and understanding among you?"

_____

_____

_____

How can a person become wise?

_____

_____

_____

_____

What is the difference between earthly wisdom and heavenly wisdom?

_____

_____

_____

_____

How is humility related to being wise?

_____

_____

_____

_____

Describe the results of heavenly wisdom demonstrated:

_____

_____

_____

_____

From 2 Corinthians 10:1–11, would you consider Paul to have been a powerful person? If so, why?

_____

_____

_____

How do you tend to view powerful people, inside the church or out of the church?

_____

_____

_____

_____

How does Paul demonstrate in this passage that his gentleness is not a sign of weakness or being timid?

_____

_____

_____

_____

Where does Paul acknowledge that his power is coming from?

_____

_____

_____

Does it seem to make a distinction between "meekness" and "gentleness"? If so, explain:

_____

_____

_____

_____

What are the principles of gentleness which you have learned from the study of these passages?

_____

_____

_____

_____

ASSIGNMENT:

• In your own words, write a profile of what a Christian with this fruit of the Spirit evident in their living, would be like:

_____

_____

_____

_____

_____

• How do you plan to apply the lessons you have learned on gentleness to your own lifestyle?

_____

_____

_____

_____

IN SUMMARY

Alexander Maclaren, noted London clergyman of the late 19th century, wrote some immortal words about our subject:

> GENTLENESS is the strongest force in the world, and the soldiers of Christ are to be priests and to fight the battle of the kingdom, robed not in jingling shining armor or with sharp swords, nor with fierce and eager bitterness of controversy, but in the meekness which overcomes. You take all the steam hammers that were ever forged and battle at an iceberg, and except for the comparatively little heat that is developed by the blows and melts some small portion, it will be ice still, though pulverized instead of whole. But let it move gently down to the southward, there the sunbeams smite the coldness to death, and it is dissipated in the warm ocean. MEEKNESS IS CONQUERING!

The Bible makes interesting analogies of how we are to exhibit and apply the fruit of gentleness. This is to be much more than just a theory of behavior which we are to talk about and teach others about. It's to be a lifestyle, it's another harvest of special fruit especially for others. Paul has written about specific applications of this fruit. It goes without saying that gentleness is to mark the Christian at all times, but there are at least the following three specific encouragements with three specific needs.

First, we are to show gentleness with spiritual babies: Paul the writer describes his ministry to the young church at Thessalonica as being "gentle among you, like a mother caring for her little children" (1 Thess. 2:7). This is a picture we can all identify with — a mother caring. A better translation would have been that the mother was "nursing" her child. There is something wrong in the family when we treat the newly born harshly. Yes, there are spiritual babies and they are not to remain in that condition. But in order to mature and develop, babies require special care. It's the truly strong Christian who can be gentle just because they have become strong. Note this admonition, "We who are strong ought to bear with the failings of the weak and not to please ourselves" (Rom. 15:1). Every one of us can be gentle!

Second, we are to serve as a nurse to the spiritually sick. There is a physical sickness as well as a spiritual sickness. Face it, some among us are sick and need a combination of firmness and gentleness in helping them back to health. There may be a problem in that some sickly Christians exhibit their condition by being touchy or having little or no appetite for the things of God. Again, Paul writes about this responsibility: "The Lord's servant must not quarrel; instead, he must be kind to everyone, able to teach, not resentful" (2 Tim. 2:24). It's with some of these folks that the soothing touch and the kindly word can work wonders. This is not putting another down or quenching the Spirit — it's an expression of this fruit at work.

Third, we are to be gentle as a craftsman with his work: What a delight it is to watch a true craftsman at work — likewise, we are called to deal with people with the touch of a skilled craftsman. Jesus Christ supplied some of the best examples of this ministry in action — the woman at the well, the father of Jairus, or with Peter after his betrayal. "But the wisdom that comes from heaven is first of all pure; then peace loving, considerate, submissive, full of mercy and good fruit, impartial and sincere" (James 3:17). It is wise to be gentle!

Here's another example of gentle kindness in action. Eight times the Ministry of Education in East Germany said "No," to Uwe Holmer's children when they tried to enroll at the university in East Berlin. The Ministry of Education doesn't usually give reasons for its rejection of applications for enrollment. But in this case the reason wasn't hard to guess. Uwe Holmer, the father of the eight applicants, is a Lutheran pastor at Lobetal, a suburb of East Berlin.

For 26 years the Ministry of Education was headed by Margot Honecker, wife of East Germany's premier, Erich Honecker. When the Berlin Wall cracked, Honecker and his wife were unceremoniously dismissed from office. He is now under indictment for criminal activities during his tenure as premier.

At the end of January the Honeckers were evicted from their luxurious palace in Vandlitz, an exclusive suburb of palatial homes reserved for the VIPs in the party. The Honeckers suddenly found themselves friendless, without resources, and with no place to go. None of their former cronies showed them any of the humanitarianism Communists boast about. No one wanted to identify with the Honeckers.

Enter Uwe Holmer. Remembering the words of Jesus, "If someone strikes you on the right cheek, turn to him the other also," Holmer extended an invitation to the Honeckers to stay with his family in the parsonage of the parish church in Lobetal.

Pastor Holmer has not reported that the Honeckers have renounced their atheism and professed faith in Jesus as Savior and Lord. But at least they fold their hands and bow their heads when the family prays

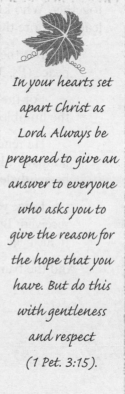

In your hearts set apart Christ as Lord. Always be prepared to give an answer to everyone who asks you to give the reason for the hope that you have. But do this with gentleness and respect

(1 Pet. 3:15).

together. Who knows what the Holmer's faith-in-action plan will lead to before this extraordinary episode ends?[1]

> But the meek will inherit the land and enjoy great peace (Ps. 37:11).

> For the Lord takes delight in his people; he crowns the humble with salvation (Ps. 149:4).

> He tends his flock like a shepherd: He gathers the lambs in his arms and carries them close to his heart; he gently leads those that have young (Isa. 40:11).

> I urge you to live a life worthy of the calling you have received. Be completely humble and GENTLE; be patient, bearing with one another in love (Eph. 4:1–2).

And the fruit of the Spirit is . . . GENTLENESS!

1. Joel C. Gerlach, "The Northwestern Lutheran," *Leadership*, Winter 1991.

Nine Fruits of the Spirit

Study Series includes

Love

Joy

Peace

Patience

Kindness

Goodness

Faithfulness

Gentleness

Self-Control

Robert Strand

Retired from a 40-year ministry career with the Assemblies of God, this "pastor's pastor" is adding to his reputation as a prolific author. The creator of the fabulously successful Moments to Give series (over one million in print), Strand travels extensively, gathering research for his books and mentoring pastors. He and his wife, Donna, live in Springfield, Missouri. They have four children.

Rev. Strand is a graduate of North Central Bible College with a degree in theology.